POSITIVE DISCIPLINE

*The Best Methods And The Best Techniques Of
Positive Discipline For Parents.
How To Eliminate Unruly Behavior In The Workplace
And Achieve Great Results*

Bart Anderson

TABLE OF CONTENTS

INTRODUCTION

Positive Discipline is a teaching method that helps children grow, provides them with the knowledge they need to understand, and encourages them to improve. Children's rights to healthy development, security from abuse, and active participation in their education are upheld. Constructive training is not permissively, approval, or lack of rules, limitations, or learners' standards. Positive Discipline is about sustainable solutions that improve the self-discipline and lifelong learning of learners. The interaction is clear and consistent; the goals, guidelines, and limits continually are reinforced. Positive Discipline is a template of the school and parental Discipline, which relies on constructive behavioral characteristics based on the idea that kids are not evil, just excellent and destructive behaviors. It is also called "social reinforcement." You should teach and improve good behaviors without verbally or physically harming the infant. Those with good behavior do not ignore issues. Alternatively, they help their children learn how to deal more effectively with problems while being calm, polite, and supportive of the baby.

A variety of strategies that, if incorporated, may help parents control their actions or educators to handle groups of students are included in a constructive discipline. Some are mentioned below. A formal, open-ended template, which many parents and schools adopt, is positive behavior intervention (PBS). This facilitates good decision-making, develops early childhood values, and supports positive behavior. I discovered Positive Discipline when I experienced the need for a new way to raise my teenage son.

Dr. Jane Nelsen's Positive Training plan. It is focused on Alfred Adler and Rudolf Dreikur's research and seeks to teach young people how to take care of their families ' duties, trust, and wealth. Positive Discipline teaches social and life skills to children and adults (including parents, teachers, childcare professionals, young people, etc.), and it is highly respectful and encouraging.

Recent research shows that children are hardwired from the beginning and are less likely to be misbehaved if connected with their community, family, and school. To succeed, children must develop the necessary social and living skills to contribute to their society. Positive training is based on an understanding of the need to practice the skill.

CHAPTER 1: BACKGROUND OF POSITIVE DISCIPLINE

The Positive Discipline Parental and Classroom Leadership Model were based on Alfred Adler and Rudolf Dreikurs. Dr. Adler first brought the concept of parental instruction to United States audiences in the 1920s. He promoted raising children respectfully, but he claimed that spoiling and pampering children were not conducive for them and culminated in emotional and behavioral problems. The classroom techniques, which were initially introduced in Vienna in the early 1920s, were brought to the United States by Dr. Dreikurs in the late 1930s. Dreikurs and Adler refer to teaching and parenting as "democratic" in a kind and firm way.

Lynn Lott, Jane Nelsen, and John Taylor collaborated in a seminar in the '80s.2 In his first teaching handbook, Lynn began training students and writing the first teaching parenting handbook (with his staff's aid). Jane was the Project Director for ACCEPT, a federally financed program, which achieved an outstanding reputation during its development phase. Jane was also responsible for Adlerian guidance principles to teachers and parents. In 1981 Jane wrote the Positive Discipline and published it herself. In 1987, Ballantine published it. In 1988, Jane and Lynn decided to collaborate in the book called The Positive Teenagers ' Discipline and began teaching parenting and management skills. Lynn and Jane both published Positive Discipline in the classroom and produced a textbook full of instructor and student experience.

The Positive Discipline series has grown in years to include titles covering various ages, family situations, and unique situations and trained Certified Positive Discipline Associates to teach Positive Discipline to schools, parents, and parent-teachers. Members, parents, and teachers of the family are empowered to become professional facilitators and communicate constructive learning ideas with their classes.

Parent training classes in a constructive discipline are offered nation-wide, and the Constructive field is widely used in social, spiritual, and public elementary schools in a classroom management method. There is already a presentation school project.

Evidence of Positive Discipline

A systematic assessment is just beginning to equate successful schools to schools that use other discipline programs. Nonetheless, tests of the application of positive discipline methods found that complementary discipline resources produce actual results. A four-year review of the school-wide introduction in lower-income primary school Sacramento found that suspensions have declined (64 to 4 per year), students have recorded violence (24 incidents to 2), and changes in the class environment, conduct, behavior, and academic performance.

Research on parents and teacher education systems of parents and teachers of pupils with "maladaptive" conduct that incorporated Positive Discipline instruments found that pupils' performance in system schools has changed statistically significantly relative with schools in control. (Nelsen, 1979) Positive results were also shown in limited trials investigating the effectiveness of different Positive Discipline methods. Studies have shown on a repeat basis that the perception of students being in the school ("connected" to school) reduces the incidence of risky social conduct (like emotional distress, suicide, etc.) (Browning, 2000, Potter, 1999; Esquivel).

There is also strong evidence that social skills teaching to young students has a protective and sustainable impact on teenagers

(Resnick et al., 1997; Battistich, 1999; Goodenow, 1993). Socially trained students are more likely to succeed at school and less likely to engage in problem behavior. While the Positive Study Parenting Program is being studied early on, Positive Discipline similar studies have been studied and have proven to be effective in changing parent behavior (Kellam et al., 1998; Battistich, 1999).

Stanley (1978) found that parents had more problems resolving their teens and were fewer autocrats in their decision-making, studying Adlerian parent education classes for teenager parents. Parents learn the skills to be both kind and firm at the same time. Positive Discipline: Many studies show that adolescents who consider both their parents' type (responsive) and company (demanding) are less likely to smoke, use marijuana, use alcohol, be violent, and start sexual activity later. The view of teens as a mother (small and company or autocrat or permissive) was associated with a better academic performance by other research.

Positive Discipline is a curriculum designed to teach young people how to make their families accountable, cooperative, and resourceful. It teaches essential social and life skills in a way that is profoundly responsible and encouraging to both children and adults (including parents, teachers, child care providers, youngsters, and others) based on the best-selling books Positive Discipline by Dr. Jane Nelsen, Lynn Lott, Cheryl Erwin, Kate Ortolano, Mary Hughes, Mike Brock, Lisa Larson, and others.

Recent research shows that kids are "hardwired" from birth to attachment and that kids who feel connected with their neighborhoods, their family, and schools are less prone to misbehave. For excel, kids have to develop the necessary social and life skills to contribute to their society. Positive Discipline is based on a knowledge of how to teach Discipline and how Discipline teaches.

Five Criteria for Effective Discipline

- It helps children feel connectedness. (Belonging and significance)

- Is mutually respectful and encouraging. (Kind and firm at the same time)
- It is effective long-term. (Considers what the child is thinking, feeling, learning, and deciding about himself and his world—and what to do in the future to survive or thrive).
- Teaches essential social and life skills. (Respect, empathy for others, problem-solving, and teamwork as well as the abilities to contribute to the family, school, or broader community)
- Invites kids to learn how competent they are. (Encourages the productive usage of personal control and independence

The principles for effective parental and classroom leadership aim at developing relationships with each other that are mutually respectful. Adults were advised in Positive Discipline to practice compassion and steadfastness at the same time.

Positive learning methods and definitions include:

Common value. Adults model firmness through concern for themselves and their interests and friendliness through consideration for the child's needs.

The idea behind the action is established. Effective Discipline acknowledges why children do what they do and work to change their faith instead of merely reversing their behavior.

- Efficient contact and expertise in troubleshooting.
- Practice training (not permissive or punitive).
- It is focusing rather than retribution on remedies.

Encouragement (rather than commendation). Fostering commitment and progress does not only achieve success but also creates long-term self-esteem and confidence.

Standard features of the Positive Discipline Model may include:

- We are training parents and adolescents through experiential activities.
- Provide opportunities to develop different techniques and to have fun learning by doing.
- Classroom discipline programs and parent education programs
- that are consistent. Parents, teachers, and childcare providers can work
- together to provide a secure, consistent environment for children.
- Continuous education and support so that communities can learn skills for each other. Positive Discipline.
- Country-wide, certified trainers can work in communities and schools.

Principles of Positive Discipline

Five components of Positive Discipline:

- Identify long-term goals
- Warmth and framework arrangement
- Child Development Knowledge
- Human variations classification
- Problem-solving and responding with Positive Discipline.

Children's rights and pedagogical principles are the basis of positive Discipline.

Identifying Long-Term Goals

To teach children everything they need to learn to succeed in their lives is one of the essential jobs in the world. However, a lot of teachers start a new school year without thinking about their future lives. They tend to concentrate on short-term goals — do your research and stop talking. Short-term circumstances can cause frustration and pressure. The problem is that we often interfere with our long-term targets by reacting to short-term stress. Teachers can respond quickly to short-term anger by shouting, insulting, or punching, and can obstruct their long-term goals.

You lose the chance to explain better results to your learners and to increase confidence and inspiration each moment that you respond this way. Teachers want students to be trustworthy, caring, inspired, responsible, and non-violent. Yelling, insulting, and abusing the pupils can show only the reverse of what they want to know. This is one of the most difficult challenges for educators—handling short-term pressure to help them achieve long-term goals. Education aims to educate pupils for adult life. We will make short-term struggles an opportunity to meet our long-term goals by teaching kids how to manage stress, to value themselves and others, and to excel in education.

Warmth and Framework Arrangement

Your long-term priorities are your intentions. You focus on how you want your students to be affected. To accomplish these aims, heat and stability need two ways.

Warmth. Warmth impacts university students psychologically and comports mentally. As educators and parents, we are encouraged to learn from our mistakes every time our friends help us. Students always learn best when they feel respected, comprehended, comfortable, and protected. The hot climate in the classroom provides the basis for your long-term goals.

Students feel comfortable in warm conditions to make errors that are essential elements of education. Students are also far more likely to work together and have fewer problems with behavior. Your academic achievement fuels your interest, making them less distractible. You don't worry, so you're less restless. Yet, they mix positive feelings with the school, and their love of learning grows.

Teachers heat their pupils, showing concern for who they are, remembering their accomplishments and contributions, and discussing circumstances from their learners' perspectives.

Structure. To accomplish college and actions, the system is the knowledge and resources that students require. It provides the learners the help they need if you are not there to solve problems. Structure teaches participants how to interact constructively, non-violently with other men. It also shows them how academically they will excel.

Once students know their goals, they become more confident in their ability to learn and trust that they will receive the information they need for their objectives. We are less distracted and less irritated so that they can concentrate on reading. Their success makes them feel good about the school and the topic they teach. We are changing their behavior.

Teachers organize their learners by serving as guides and examples to positive role models, discussing the reasoning for the guidelines, encouraging students to set rules, learning their opinions, motivating them to find ways of correcting errors that enable them to know, to be equal and to control their frustration and to prevent attacks.

Positive learning incorporates energy and order during the school years of each child. This lets educators accomplish their short-term goals, thus impacting their pupils for a long time. It is a way of thinking. It also increases students' interest in learning, strengthens their drive for academic success, and promotes it.

Child Development Knowledge

Teachers know that as children grow, children are changing. Development is a phase that is relentless and never stopping. We can teach children new information and skills because they change. Every learning builds on previous knowledge–and provides the basis for future learning. Nevertheless, kids at every level do not know the same way.

Their approaches to thought and understanding change, so we must also change the way we teach them. You need to provide heat and stability that suits your students ' stage of development to achieve your longer-term objectives. Attendees must balance the skills of participants. We will start to understand the cause of their behavior as we try to see the world through the eyes of an a6-year old or a 13-year-old. We can then be more successful educators.

Early childhood.   Many of the creations of children and educators are unseen. Pre-school experiences set the stage for their ability to know, their enthusiasm for education, and their social interaction abilities. Often, in what children learned about themselves years before, the learning and behavioral difficulties become clear at school.

Teachers need to understand how the perception of a child's childhood could have formed a self-concept reflected in their learning attitudes and behavior in the classroom or the community.

Developments During School Life. It is one of the most significant changes she ever will make. School is an entirely new environment from a child's point of view. It is in a new place filled with new children and new adults. New plans and procedures are to be pursued. And the infant may be without their family or guardians for the first time. It poses the kid with a huge challenge.

Teachers bear a large proportion of liability for the lively child's adjustment at the point of school admission. We will affect the attitudes of children in school and in education for many years to come. Teachers will help kids change this when they realize how kids think at this age. Children experience events that have not yet been learned at the point of school admission. Kids at this level can grasp conceptual terms but find it challenging to comprehend and understand abstract concepts that any situation exists in more than one form. We focus on the thing we frequently like, which cannot include the less evident at the same time.

He is likely to feel excluded when a child of this age is disciplined. Throughout school settings, students are uncomfortable and nervous because children feel their educators condemn them. Upon response, they may remove–or act—children whose age is quiet, shy, and fearful of making mistakes. So, teachers are more anxious as they respond to criticism. We will quickly lose motivation to try over time. Kids who act up will be disciplined again, which will lead to increased anxiety. These kids can't concentrate and start to fail in their schoolwork. We will stop caring about school over time.

If a child has trouble transitioning to school, they must review their actions and discover its causes. We can then choose a response that helps the child to learn and to develop self-discipline.

During early primary school (6-8 years). During this period, children are usually keen to learn and highly motivated to face new obstacles once the transfer to school has been successful. You have an inherent effort to understand the universe. During later years, children's interactions during elementary education have set the stage for progress. Teachers now need to create a climate for education that embraces and inspires children to learn. Some aspects of children will threaten the development of a supportive environment at this level. They are willing, interested, busy, and self-employed.

Late Primary (9- to 12-year-olds). In late primary schools, kids can creatively solve problems, and their analytical skills will quickly improve. You can also find your feelings (metacognition). This ensures you will talk about how you read, assess your approaches, and test new ones. Kids actively rely on peer interactions. They shape close friendships–and they can be deeply contradictory. Teachers must build a learning environment on encouraging at this level.

Teenagers (13- to 18- year-olds). Youth is a period for significant change. Young people cross the bridge between childhood and adulthood, a dramatic shift in all its growth fields. The kid should think hypothetically-they should logically solve questions, formulate theories, and routinely evaluate them. We talk about' big problems,' for instance, economics and culture. You might challenge the reasoning of adults. It is not a sign of disrespect; it is a sign that you can think and figure out your worth and faith.

Teenagers struggle to achieve an identity sense. Their intense determination, motivation, their need for peer support, and their hard time recognizing the dangers will contribute to repeated disagreements with parents and teachers. Attempts to control or force them to take those positions can cause resentment and poor contact. We will be embarrassed by physical punishment and very pessimistic about their attitude to class.

Professionals must help students develop a sense of right and wrong and a sense of responsibility and skill. Confidence is critical listening, providing transparent and honest details; clear expectations and framework are so essential.

Human Variations Classification

While all children experience the same developmental stages, they endure this in various environments, communities, attitudes, skills, and skills. Every class consists of a group of students with their own stories every. Through their courses,' students need to know the different story's.

Problems Solving and Responding with Positive Discipline. That child comes into the classroom with its own unique experience. Teachers need to understand and provide the support they need to understand the challenges faced by each child. A teacher who believes in it can differ between its success and school failure for students who feel "different." I am here at the teacher's secret. I am there for teachers ' sakes. "Isn't she going to stop speaking?" Why can't his homework just be done?

Once an educator has established her long-term goals, understands the importance of bringing comfort, order, acknowledging child growth, and recognizing individual differences, it will be motivated by constructive training to overcome such problems.

Recall that a participant must have confidence, comprehension, and security. There's no pain to training. In difficult situations, it is not always possible to respond constructively. Thought and training were conducted with constructive direction.

Both teachers ' relationships with their pupils can be driven by a constructive approach rather than the difficult ones. It can also direct educational instruction, not just social skills and behavior. The strategy and the answer are essential to think ahead—training, training, and training.

CHAPTER 2: PARENTING AND POSITIVE DISCIPLINE

The most important job that you ever have is to be a parent! Not only your child but you, as a person, are affected by parenting. There are a lot of rewards and challenges to parenting. You will affect the individual your child is. You get many smiles and hugs and kisses. You always laugh, play, see your child grow and grow. They will also often question why they said the right thing or if you could instead have said it.

Parents appreciate and want the best for their children. Yet kids don't come with orders and don't always respond or follow as you wish. Once you think you have sorted out stuff, your infant often transitions into a different development stage, and what worked before is not going to work anymore. You will find new joy and obstacles to the new location.

Practicing Positive Discipline

A Handbook for Parents can help you learn from your child's early grade years and provide you with tools to help with typical parenting interactions. It is not desirable to stretch. Spanking is not beneficial to positive outcomes and can contribute to other difficulties.

Kids are driven by other strategies than spanking usually have better mental health, feel better, and are less anxious. What we're trying to achieve is good health. Many different approaches promote positive growth and help children understand how to manage themselves, what is planned, and how they behave correctly.

In your neighborhood and area, there are many other resources available that can assist you with a healthy discipline— the physician and tutor of your son, the public health care provider, the CEE, and the early baby and family instructor, to name a few.

Parenting is a skill that has been experienced. Citizens get their thoughts about spreading their learning, books, journals, newspapers, the Web, tv, seminars, physicians, and other family members and friends. As a mother, you need to monitor and identify approaches and resources that work best for you and your son. The aim is to become the best parent.

Discipline Is Teaching. The domain is the Latin word discipline, which implies "to instruct." You are an educator as a mother. You can help them learn the way you discipline your children. The domain allows children to understand who they want when they act and when they behave wrongly. Discipline helps children to control their conduct.

They were nurturing your child. Promoting is where the most effort you have to make. Once children know that they are loved and supported, they learn best. Here are some ideas:

- Love your kids, whatever they do.
- Listen to your children. Listen to your children.
- Ask them when they're fine.
- Wait for your kids for the best.
- Make sure that they are both emotionally and physically secure.
- Be a model of the right role.

Guide Your Child

Kids need to help them understand the actions you expect of them and the laws you anticipate. You also need guidance with controlling the emotions, knowing accountability, and discovering how to control yourself. If rules are broken, your child needs to know what will happen.

- Help your child discover solutions to the problems. Here are some suggestions.
- Teach your kid how things can be done.
- Save your child from circumstances that your child can't cope with.
- Support your child with learning how to calm.
- Plan for difficult situations for your son.
- If you can answer "yes," "no," whether appropriate.
- Give your child the chance to do it in the right direction.

Reacting to Your Child's Misconduct

There is usually a reason why kids are misbehaved. We can be exhausted, thirsty, irritated, vigilant, or reluctant. If you can find out what causes this misconduct, you will respond more successfully to the misconduct and avoid the behavior. They have to worry about what triggers the outburst, for instance, if you always witness your 7-year-old breakdown when you get back from the class. The will may be tired and hungry or something at school upsetting. Learn how school works for educators. Consider a nutritious snack to help your children make the transition from school to home and provide some time to read or play a game. Other strategies to consider:

- Take away the privilege by giving the child a job to do.
- Tell your child clearly that it was not acceptable to do what he or she did.
- When something is hurt, expect a new one or help pay for the new one from the family.
- Make sure that children experience the impact of their actions securely.

What Does Penalties Mean

A consequence is a person's doing something. When kids are mis conforming, parents must respond to understand the consequences of their actions, and the next time, they prepare accordingly.

As a result, a child should be allowed to be forgiven. The product is better than pain, fear, shame, or humiliation. Families have to determine whether they have to behave objectively or instinctively. A rational example: a kid is on a wall painting — the child helps clean the wall. An example of a natural result: a child will refuse to eat dinner— the child will be starving afterward.

Babies – Birth to 18 Months

Kids are primed for learning and growing in the country.

By all their senses, babies know. We also touch the things around them with their eyes.

- Babies learn to speak by listening to the people in their life and talking to them.
- Babies use screaming for things to say to you.
- Babies must be cherished, protected, and healthy.
- Parents need to understand that babies explore their world and learn how others react to it. Babies are not deliberately misbehaving–they are just curious!

What should Parents know about Discipline for their baby?

- Give a lot of love to your baby. Remember, with too much love, and you can't spoil a child.
- Do not move the kid or shake it.
- Push the kid into areas that aren't all right when he or she comes in.
- Out of your baby's reach, but dangerous things.
- If your baby wants anything wrong with the children, send something all right.

- Try regular routines, particularly for eating and sleeping, for your baby's day.
- Figure out a way to take a rest if you are exhausted or if things go too far for you.

Be Confident as Parent

This takes time for your new baby to sound. You will meet each other and your kid. It's different for each baby. It takes time to learn how to feed, sleep, and care for your child. Live as easy as you can with your days. Consider talking to a friend, family member, or a loving person regularly. Call your kid's doctor or call one of these numbers at the back of this newsletter if you feel inadequate, uncertain, or frustrated.

What is Attachment

Attachment is a strong feeling for each other between parents and children. Most children are confident and concerned with robust and secure attachments with their parents and other significant adults in their lives.

When They Cry

The way your baby talks to you is crying. Your kid will call due to:

- Fatigue
- Disease
- Solitude
- Wet piping
- Being overwhelmed by people
- Stomach gas
- Being too warm or too cold
- Need your love and attention

Parent Guide

It's not possible to spoil a kid. Once taken up and comforted, an infant always screams less. You can't hold a baby too much and comfort him. The kid begins to believe you and that if appropriate, you will be there. You will know what the crying of your baby tells you with practice.

You need to do the best to keep composure when a child screams and talks. Try to find out first when the kid weeps.

- Try to "swaddle" your baby into a blanket, wrap your baby-friendly, and close your baby.
- Give yourself a few minutes to relax. Put your baby, like a side-up crib, in a safe place. Then go to the house somewhere where you can't hear the cries until you feel calmer.
- Put your child in a built-in park.
- Take your child for a car ride.
- Seek to "wear" the harness or baby carrier for your kid. The breathing and body motions will help a baby comfortable.
- Seek to sway or sing gently to your kid.
- Call a friend.

Often when the problem is understood and what helps weeping stops. While you might sound like your baby trembling or spanking, it is never all right. The corpses of babies are very poor. Shaking or picking up will badly hurt and even destroy your kid.

Sleep Discipline of Newborn

Most newborns don't sleep all night. Many kids don't always sleep all night until they're 6-9 months old. It may be essential to eat, alter, and reassure your newborn child regularly. Enjoy your new baby in this peaceful time. Your baby doesn't try to make life hard.

Sleep Discipline of 3-Month-Old

By looking at the toys over the crib or playing rattles, babies can entertain themselves. They can spend three or four hours between the supplies and last longer sleep during the night.

- Ensure your baby gets enough to eat during the day to help your baby sleep for more extended periods during the night.
- Try to increase your last pre-bed meal.
- Keep attention low in the middle of the night. Feed your baby or adjust the discomfort if it is sticky or soiled.

The risk of Sudden Infant Death Syndrome (SIDS) is minimized when placing infants on their sides. Ensure that the bed is sturdy and closely suits the crib. Put quilts, pillows, and cozy baby items forward. Use your crib rather than the sheet to protect your infant. Do not put your baby on a sofa, soft mattress, waterbed or pillow, or another sleeping surface.

Sleep Discipline of 7-Month-Old

The baby started to calm down when they were in pain and settle down when they were sleepy at 7 or 8 months. Nevertheless, these results must have to be dealt with. If you can never rest or recover independently, you would probably rely upon other people to fall asleep.

Help your baby find a way to sleep comfortably and without your assistance. Maybe one of the below would like to apply.

- Swing by the crèche of your son. You don't have the kid to pick up.
- Hug your kid softly.
- Speak with the son. The baby knows the tone of your voice is all right, and it is time to sleep.
- have a relaxing ritual with a soothing tub, a photo book, music, rocking, or singing. •
- As part of the bedtime routine, offer hugs and kisses.

Call the doctor for your child or contact one of the numbers in the back of this brochure if you need any more information. When they are 7 to 8 months old, most babies start to spend time in which only people they know very much want to be around. Understand that your kid has to be with people with confidence. Let your baby feel in control to get used to new people. Don't pressure your kid into being carried by a human that the baby isn't accepted. Show your kid that by understanding the baby's worries, you are a haven.

Toddlers – 18 Months to 3 Years

All children become independent and know the world in which they live.

- All children must discover, run, climb, taste, and touch.
- When you try to stop them, they may get mad.
- Kids know what they want, and they're going to say to you. If you don't grasp the vocabulary, you can become irritated.
- Children see and imitate what others do. You will do what you, other family members, and TV or movie protagonists say.
- Toddlers have their brains, but they need guidance to frustrate them, and they need to defend against risk.
- Disciplining children means training them to control, eat, hop, ride, and scale their urges.

Steps to Positive Discipline of Toddlers

- Show lots of love to your kid.
- Find material to say yes.
- Remember that your kid is content with good behavior.
- Do not spit or shake your kid.
- Out of control of your child's position, dangerous things.
- When kids want something they can't have, feel sorry for or disappointed and involve them in something they can get.
- Seek to have your day's routine.
- Parents must always be involved in the development of babies as "breaks."
- Give yourself a break from parenting when you get stressed, or issues become too much for you.
- Tell yourself if your child was mistaken or just trying to learn more.

- If the child's behavior has been an a' lousy call,' please admit your mistake and apologize.
- Practice the child's style of behaving. When you scream, your child will talk.
- Make sure you have the focus on your child. When you request your child to do something, be precise and prompt.
- Be realistic about the independence of your child.

Trying to Do Everything

You require kids at all times to be with them.

You undoubtedly see kids getting into it all. Children have the job of discovering their universe. That's how kids learn.

There are a few ways to make your home safe for your kids: • Bring out of reach of your child ruptured or dangerous objects, like electric cords.

- I am using electrical socket security covers.
- On cabinets and drawers, put safety locks.
- Avoid stairway security doors and non-safe rooms.
- Under tables move seats.
- You should expect your child to get angry when you take anything dangerous away. Try to offer a safe toy for distraction.

Why Childproof

It should be assured that kids travel comfortably wherever they go. All around them, kids will learn. You are going to touch, taste, roll, poke, and check everything you can see. That's how kids learn. Enable them to discover items that should not be beyond their control securely. They will start to teach older children not to handle other things.

Policy on TV

To grow and thrive, children must always investigate their world. Children should not watch TV under two years of age. TV is an inactive operation. Television does not involve children in active learning, moving, and playing process with others. TV is an addiction, so parents have to try hard to limit their exposure to television. Include other children-related activities such as workshops, art projects, or outdoor sports.

Children are curious about what you do on the fireplace. Pull away your child and say, "No, the oven is hot and will hurt you," rather than hanging your hands or shouting. Children learn that issues are unstable because you remind them over and over.

- Remove the child from an insecure place or item while waiting for learning to take place.
- Seek to get the kid involved in something else, including plastic bowls, pan lids, and timber spoons.
- Have your kid in the kitchen, a safe place to run.

You've heard this a lot if you have a kid.

Typically, "I do it," unless you're in a rush, is an issue. Encourage the freedom of your son. Put your clothes, brush your teeth, and get into a seat in your vehicle. You have to allow extra time to do these chores for your son, but the more you prepare, the quicker your child can do this stuff and save you time afterward.

Tantrums

Tantrum is usually caused by the tiredness, drought, rage, or disappointment of an infant. Your little child might shut her eyes, close her fists, and shout. He might run, leap to the floor and make a real scene.

Take the time to avoid tangles. Make sure your child sleeps well. If your child is tired or weary, stop taking your child anywhere. If you have no option, carry your child's healthy snacks, magazines, favorite games, pencils, and paper to protect it from boredom. Why is tannic at this era so common?

- Curious kids. You don't know why you can't always reach, feel, and experience all about you.

- Kids can't usually tell you what they want in letters. We may be upset with that.
- If kids are hungry, sleepy, warm, anxious, or want attention, they often respond with strong emotions.

Tantra is natural. Tantra is usual. Allow your child to have the tantrum while it is quiet, and nobody else is harmed. Make sure your child knows that he's sad.

- Stay calm and ignore the tantrum when you're at home.
- Stay calm and remove the child when in a public place. Take a restful position so your child will relax.
- Many kids find it difficult to calm down.
- Take your child gently, speak quietly, and clarify that all will be all right.
- So wherever you are, if you react peacefully, the tantrum should stop sooner.

If a child is in a public spot and has a tantrum, you might be tempted to avoid a scene by giving a child what they want. As adults do that, children learn that if they jump and scream, and you have more tanning in the future, they're having what they want.

Another approach to control the actions of a little kid is to channel the child's interest elsewhere. Give your baby a fun toy to play with if you want something you don't want. Take your child to another part of the room if you switch to an open stairway.

They Think They Are Boss

Kids begin to know at age two that they can do such tasks by themselves. You're curious about and want to use your new skills!

Here are a few strategies to assist you and your child in learning new skills: Say, "Would you like to run today, or do you want to move in the shopping cart?"• Schedule extra time to allow your child to do stuff autonomously. You and your child can feel less pressure.

- Allow children to be alone in their car seats.

- Ask if assistance is required.
- Keep to core laws. Your child is safe then and knows what to expect. Children will sit in a car seat, for example; it's not an option.

The baby continues to test new skills and wants control. Parents are rushed and want power as well. Parents must have empathy for kids and provide them with opportunities to understand how they affect their world. They must be careful with them. Nonetheless, you have to tell "no" to your child's safety at times, such as, "If we cross the street, you have to hold my hand."

Biting

Bite, strike, and attack many kids are very popular for babies. The effect can be babies nervous and over-stimulated and chewing. When parents respond enthusiastically, a child can learn to bite to be conscious.

- Watch the infant look for signs of overstimulation. Here are a few ways to prevent biting. Take the problem from your child and make it relax.
- Kids are angry and frustrated when they're sick of being hungry. If it does arise often, try to change your child's feeding and sleep routine or keep your child apart from other children.
- Treat the bitten child with love.
- Chat about different ideas and suggestions with others who matter to your son.
- Try learning what the biting did. Young children have little ability to solve other children's problems.

If your kid bites, tell the kid that it's not fair to bit and separate the kid from the other children. Help your childcare about how the other child feels and think about ways to say "sorry." This does not teach a child to stop biting and may intensify biting.

Toilet Training

You should encourage the instruction of toilets, but do not pressure them. Often before their son, parents are ready to be taught toilets. If:

- Your child tells you, "I need to take the bathroom." Your kid is ready to start the toilet teaching.
- The muddy or soiled discomfort is what the kid tells you.

Until they are about three years of age, many kids do not recognize their "need to go." A two-year-old may start teaching toilets but cannot be fully trained until he is three years old or older. Do not threaten or embarrass a wetting, soiling, or underwear boy. This can make your child feel unwilling about something uncontrollable and can cause toilet instruction to take longer.

An infant will typically begin to learn about toilets at the age of two.

- Most kids will stay dry until they reach age three-and-a-half but not all.
- Most kids become clean by the age of five, but not all, during nap and night.

Sharing

Many two-year-olds don't grasp sharing. Until the age of three or four, your child will not be able to understand sharing. The more you advocate for cooperation at age two, the greater the disappointment and anger your child will feel.

- Praise your child for sharing. This is what you can do.
- Learn how to interact with your child by sharing some of your things.
- Make sure that there are plenty of items for all ages to use when children play together.
- It is a good thing that your kid can start to catch this part.

Kids should go through a period if one parent chooses the other one. But the only adult who is permitted to do something for the infant, such as putting on clothes, getting food, or getting ready for bed, can be overwhelming to a mother. Try not to make it a significant problem or to take it personally. The behavior would soon change with the support of the chosen parent and the child's continuous positive interaction with the kid.

Making A Mess

Careful monitoring is required for everyday people. All children want to touch, taste, see, and explore. This is how kids get to know their environment. Seek not to touch disorderly objects. Provide safe spaces for kids to learn.

- Children don't make angry messes. You make messes because you learn how things work. You know.
- Do not forget the mess your child has made.

This is the ideal opportunity to teach refreshing things. See how to clean up your child.

Where your youngest children are and what they do, it is essential always to know. The infant's job is to inquire. Your job is to ensure the security of your kids. Keep an eye on your baby's safety continuously.

Making Kid Sit at A Place

The children shouldn't stay still or be still for a long time! You are interested, and you have to travel and enjoy running and jumping!

Toddlers like to speak to you and others, often dramatically.

Sometimes you need to sit still and be still with your son. Here are some things you can try:

- Please bring your child something to your little one with small toys or photo books.
- Bring a snack that isn't too messy, such
- as crackers, fruit, or cheese.

- We are giving as much attention as possible to your son.
- Display things in the space to attract the attention of your son.
- Watch patty pastries or other games.
- Make sure that your child needs to sit still before active time.
- You and your child can, in certain situations, move to a place that will not disturb others.

Talk to your kid's doctor or call one of the numbers in the back of the pages when you have further questions regarding your child's development at this age.

Pre-School Kids

Students of pre-school age live today. They're curious about all they can do and learn. Children typically want to be with other kids, imagine, and want to do what older children and adults do. We want to be your daughter at the same moment.

- Preschoolers will rely, even though they don't know how, on doing something for themselves.
- Pre-school students will check the laws and comment about principles with which they disagree.
- Preschool students were fantastic! We say imaginative tales and hate the night, demons, wildlife, etc.
- Infants like to be involved and ask what to do for others.
- You are watched closely by preschoolers. We are shown far more by the acts.

What are my preschoolers' best ways to discipline?

- Give a lot of love to your child.
- Out of control of your child's position, dangerous things.
- Seek to have your day's routine.
- Ask yourself: does my child behave incorrectly or simply try to learn?

- Act the way you want your child to act.
- Be specific and direct when you ask your
- child to do something.
- Make your child honest about what he can do.
- Use your child's time, mainly when your child is responsible for playing.
- Catch that your child is right and let it know that your child has noticed you.
- Get your child ready for upsetting occasions.
- Let your kid take a break while facing a difficult time.

Be Prepared for Difficult Situations

When you dread sending your pre-school student to the hospital, grocery store, or where your child can accidentally go, here are some things to try, for instance.

- Talk to your child about your expected behavior before you go.
- Tell "You have to sit in the food cart, and not look for stuff in the supermarket
- Try not to take your child's seats if your child is exhausted or hungry.
- Carry along treats and games.
- If your child has problems while you're in the store or hospital, send a note about the laws. Please ask your child what the rules are.
- Know how proud you are when seeing good conduct to your preschooler.

Bed-Time Struggles

Setting up a bedtime routine is one of the best things you can do for yourself and your son.

- Determine when to go to bed for your kid.
- Start your routine approximately 30 minutes before bedtime.

- A bath, a light snack, brushing teeth, and storytime can be the child's routine.
- This isn't an excellent time for playing or action games.
- Try sticking every night to your schedule.

Is Your Kid Afraid of Darkness

Address their worries with your kids. The concerns of children are legitimate. Don't make fun of it or say it's not real. Put a light in the room or a tiny light in the night, or left a light on the hallway before you sleep. A special blanket or a stuffed animal makes some children feel safer.

It may also lead to having the child cope with the fear of the dark. If you first attempt a bedtime routine, it will not work correctly until the pattern is firmly established.

- The child will continue to come out of the house. Take your child back to bed with firmness and care. You might have multiple times to do that.
- Many kids are at a point where they hate the gloom. Understand that your child's apprehension is genuine, reassure, and find ways to get over it.
- Use a flashlight or illumination at night or put it in the hallway.
- Many kids need more sleep time.
- Speak with stuffed animals or let your child watch a movie.
- The child has to sleep comfortably enough. For each child, that may be different. Try finding ways to relax your son. Sing a soothing tune, or keep a stuffed animal, have your child respire gradually.
- Often shortening the afternoon nap or making it easy for your kid to sleep in the late afternoon

The Selective Eater

Bear in mind that one adult's role is for some healthy food choices and that the task of a kid is to choose what and how much to consume to prevent fried meat and make fun meals. Make meals a family time for conversation and not for punishment or pressure.

- Provide a range of colorful, colorful, and textured, healthy foods for your child.
- Put a small amount on the plate if your child does not like a new food. Tell your kid to take a bite or two. Do not force eating. Do not force eating.
- Don't demand that kids eat all their plates. This may lead to poor food behavior.
- Some kids don't like different mixed foods.
- The kid is not prepared to eat a combination.
- Many kids might complain that they are too full for a lot of their meals, but they have plenty of dessert space. To prevent dessert from being used as a reward, but rather as the last part of a meal, let your child know that it is all right to leave the table if he or she has eaten. Explain, when everyone is ready, the dessert is coming. And provide healthy food for dessert. The choices maybe peanut butter sliced apple or granola yogurt.
- Note shifts of tastes. You'll be shocked one day by your kid and the food rejected before that.

Helping You in the Kitchen

At the right age, the pre-school child is in the kitchen. Support your child to prepare and organize meals. Infants like to mix things in a pan. They can help you clean the table and put your napkins and plastic cups on your table, for instance. Help your children discover a variety of healthy options to choose from. You can learn a lot and find that your decisions are meaningful.

What Snacks to Try

Blend 100% fruit juice and sparkling water in equal parts, instead of soda pop. Bring small carrots, celery, peanut butter, banana chunks, apple slices, raisins, or clean grapes to your kid instead of candy. Give cheese or crackers rather than chips. For a cool treat, freeze 100% fruit juice in a cup of paper to produce a popsicle with a straw in the center.

- Be rational about how much food you or your kid uses. There are a few other options here. Kids do not need food aids of adult size.
- The taste buds of an infant are far more responsive than yours. Children usually don't like strong, like onions, or foods not familiar in their color or texture.
- Serving mild to hot food gives the best flavor and is better for your kid's mild language and skin.
- One day, it's normal for kids to die and have very little nutrition the next day.
- Kids were thinner than adults in their stomachs.
- You need less food at once, and you have to eat more often during the day.
- Help your child obtain necessary nutrients throughout the day with healthy snacks.
- Offer your kid water all day instead of milk, fruit juices, and other liquids at all times.
- Speak to your child's doctor if you are worried about the eating habits of your child.

Your child learns how to use utensils, drink a cup, and eat during meals. You should avoid such mealtime injuries. Use cups, knives, and dishes in child size. They are using lids for high-sided cups and pots. Help kids remain in a better eating height with booster seats. Make sure the booster seat stays secured to the chair to keep it from sliding.

Power Battles

Irritation and anger are often the first reactions of a mother when a child fails to do.

The child will do so if you get upset. Tell yourself first whether this is an important battle. If it isn't, let your child take that path. Walk away until your children calm down when it's essential. Start your petition, then. Walk away again when your daughter cries. Keep in mind that there is no alternative, and if your child does not change the behavior, you will make a difference. Offer your child a choice to avoid power struggles first and foremost. In the tub, instead of saying, "Are you ready for bed? Tell, It's time for the pool. Would you like bubbles or pure water?".

When talking to your child, use simple words. Be straightforward and specific about your wishes.

"I want you to take your block and place it in the toy box," rather than suggest, "Clean up that mess."

It is better to act sometimes than to speak. Your child has been asked to sit and eat dinner on many occasions, but your child is still running around the table. Stop saying to pull the children's plate off the table respectfully. You can have the food back when the child sits on the chair, ready to eat when the child wants to eat. The kid usually goes back to sleep and feed. You can get the kid's focus from annoying things.

You know the Emotions of Your Kids. Tell your child you recognize when you become upset, unhappy, or sad. Say, "You're upset; I can see." Sometimes it takes everything to make your child feel calmer or healthier. Recognizing feelings does not mean that you'll give in' or accept the behavior. The emotion can be identified.

What is time out? Time out implies that a child is taken away from a painful or unpleasant situation to help the kid and the adult calm down. It teaches children that it's all right to take time off if they need it. How to use the technique see the "Time Out" chapter at the rear of this booklet.

Damping the Bed

Many children will stay dry until or shortly after kindergarten during the night.

If your kid does not keep dry all night long by the age of six, visit your doctor. However, due to stress, a child may sometimes wet the bed later. If your child is upset about wetting the ground, make sure it helps correct this problem, growing bigger and older. Don't do it a lot.

- Limit drinks after dinner in the meantime.
- Avoid caffeine drinks since urination is stimulated.
- Use unwieldy undergarments.
- Put your infant on a water-proof mattress pad or take a towel to wash if it's cold.
- Make sure the bathrooms are before bed for your child.

Waking your child to the bathroom in the middle of the evening will create more anxiety than it merits. Speak to your child's physician if you're still worried.

Whining

Many kids whine if they want; many whines if they are exhausted, hungry, or overwhelmed. • If your child is crying about something you like and don't get, take a hug and say that you recognize emotions of honesty or frustration. Here are some suggestions you can do: Tell the boy, "Nobody wants to listen when you complain."

Recommend or explain ways to speak that are more strongly considered. More than once, you might need to say this.

- Stay calm and leave the scene if the moaning persists.
- Do not give in to whine, tangle, strike, or other unpleasant habits.
- When kids get what they want when they do, they are going to fight

Tell kids about their good behavior, what you like. Say, "When I am on the line, I like it softly if you talk." Lobbying and motivating work to help your kid appreciate what you intend.

Grade Schoolers: 5-9 Years Old

Grade school children think about the real world, connect with, and become more confident of other people and ideas.

- The emphasis on children of this age is very significant.
- For children of early school, friends are becoming essential.
- You must learn to talk to others, understand other children's feelings, and be a friend.
- Parents are still essential. Your child needs to help you go from home to school, to make rules to see that they are enforced. Kids require help from parents to try new things to demonstrate to them problems can be solved. They have to hear their concerns from parents.

What Are My High School Children's Best Ways to Handle Them?

- No matter what your baby's doing. Love your baby.
- Be a lovely template.
- Maintain a schedule regularly.
- Be clear on what to do and how to do with your child.
- Show your child what he or she is doing you are interested in.
- Try seeing the point of view of your son.
- Help make your point with stories.
- Welcome to review your child's rules as you grow up.
- Knock off a mistreatment right or add an extra assignment.
- Establish a system to allow your child to obtain privileges.
- Wait for children to help patch or pay for breaking things.
- Be trustworthy. Be reliable. Keep up what you're saying.
- Help your child take a break ("time out") anytime your child has trouble.
- Indicate the child's behavior and what comportments you are proud of, in particular.

When They Break Rules

Kids go through periods as they check the rules. Your child may believe some of the old practices have become too immature.

- Stay in control and relaxed. Check out the law and why. Decide whether it still suits or whether your son has forgotten the principle. Remember if your child could have violated the law and whether he or she follows the policy.
- When you decide to change a policy, clarify with your child how the law is to adjust and what if the rules are violated.
- Talk to your child about the explanation for your policy.
- Don't forget a law once your kid splits.
- Respond as quickly as possible. Make sure your response shows your child how to follow correctly and why the rule is relevant

Rules keep us safe, show us a course of action, and help us to get along. If your child violates a law, you will react in such a manner that your child can see the value of following the rule. One effective way is to make use of an effect. We have a policy that nobody will watch TV before homework is done, for instance. Before you do schoolwork, your child watches a clip. No TV is caring for a day as a result of breaking the rule. Be sure to follow through when you have clearly stated this.

Telling A Lie

Kids are dishonest because they are scared to face what they did. You may think that they will be punished, feel trapped, or believe that lying is more comfortable. Children also pass stages in which lying is more frequent.

- Make your child know that he is lying.
- Tell your kid you don't like cheating.
- Seek not to put your child in a position where the first lie leads to a second lie.
- Make sure adults are not lying in your house. Kids can do what you do more than you claim.
- Make it clear that cheating is not reasonable to your child. Love your child in a problematic situation for telling the truth.

Sibling Quarrels

Grade school children are at the age where getting along with brothers and sisters can be difficult. You want your children to get along. You want to respect and appreciate them. In your house, you want peace.

- If your sibling's clash, stay careful and figure out if anyone is injured or risky. If there are no children, tell them that they have to do it.
- Substances and personal space also cause crashes. Provide clear rules on what is to be discussed in the house and what is unique. It is the owner's responsibility to agree to share private information.
- Don't try to compare the children. Treat each child equally.
- Offer kids an opportunity to have their time split.
- Please ask your kids for suggestions on how to do it. However, you decide which of their ideas is meaningful.
- All in the house must be treated with respect and be safe.

The competition between kids is one way for kids to grasp dispute resolution. Let the kids solve the problem themselves if necessary. Move-in only if kids do not seem to work and the argument is out of control.

Foul Language

Your child is probably going to learn some foul language at school or in the press.

Children sometimes begin to use foul language.

- Let your child know that your house is not all right with cursing or curding words. You want your child to comply with this principle also in the class.
- Watch your language for yourself. You're going to copy your kid if you curse.

- Do not clean the teeth of kids out of soap or other disgusting products. This is kid abuse that shows that parents can do kids bad things.

You either stubbed the toe or struck the thumb with a hammer at times in your life. Maybe your first response was an "evil" term. Children have encounters with ordinary nature. Support the kid to use better words.

Talking Back

If your child shows no respect, it is easy to get upset. You should help your child understand not to speak and how you react to love.

- Tell your child that you want to learn, but you won't listen until you both have a chance to relax.
- Excuse your rage and scream. Excuse if you are both relaxed; tell your child specifically which specific words or tone of voice you considered inappropriate.
- That means your child learns what kind of polite behavior. Tell your kid how you're doing today. In the future, tell your kid what you intend.
- Allow trying again to your child. I hope your boy has learned from your example and apologizes, but he should not be forced to apologize.

I lost my patience before. Tell your child. I'm sorry I made you feel bad. I'm sorry. I was not polite. "I was not pleasant. We're not perfect at all. This helps children in their lives to learn to excuse themselves and others.

Spanking

Discipline is education. It is retrospective and polite. Spanking doesn't help learn; it's a penalty. Punishment is reverse and does not respect a child. Spanking teaches an infant that adults are more robust, that abuse is the way to solve problems. A tumultuous child focuses on feeling hurt and anger, not learning what has been done wrong. What are some reasons for spanking by parents?

Spanking draws praise from the kid and prevents the misconduct—at the point alone. Children do not learn what you expect from them or how to behave in the future. It also doesn't teach children how to behave because their parents do not follow the rules. Spanking is a model for parents and teachers and does not create positive feelings.

Kids cannot be harmed by spanking. Tears and tantrums have shown the kids, who are deprived, what they want. Instead of encouraging parents to learn things for themselves who abuse their kids, they still do too much for them. The best way to avoid spoilage for kids is to show them attention and set limits and specific behavior guidelines.

Tip for Parents

Imagine parental care as the child's bank account. You will deposit this account for every positive thing–embracing, celebrating, motivating, educating, and following a law. Each negative thing you do— jealousy, shame, shame— is a withdrawal from this account. To have a good relationship with your child, you need to make many more deposits than retirements.

Sometimes parents will think only of one option if the kid is incorrect. Spank. "I'm striving not to sprinkle, but there are moments when nothing else helps." When they're angry or frustrated, parents usually swing. The good news is that you can find many more ways to respond to your son's actions. Parents who continue to discipline their kids are generally more likely to work than to last.

"Punishing is one of my traditions." Punishing in different societies can be appropriate, but this does not mean that instruction and self-control are right.

Many people with children grow up to be all that. But that's not because they've been spanked. Since their parents also used many constructive forms of Discipline. Research indicates that spanking as a child can lead to problems like depression, domestic violence, and chemical abuse. Most grown-ups say they remember the times they were spanked.

Tip for Parents

Your child learns that hitting is the way to resolve problems as you stretch your son. Even if your child looks after old parents, it may continue to hit others through the lifetime!

Control Your Anger

Almost all parents know how upset you maybe if a child does not respond.

- Note, it is the actions of your family that makes you angry rather than your kids.
- Punishing and other penalties won't teach the kid to regulate themselves and what to do.
- Make sure your child can do what you want.

Families often react negatively to a child's irritating behavior due to their tiredness, anxiety, or frustration at someone or something else. In many situations, parents need to find ways to sleep better, eat better, speak to a counselor and a therapist to help them work out coping with children's frustration and actions.

How to Control Your Anger

- Save it! Stop it! —Take a while to refresh yourself. Before you discipline your child, wait until you are calm.
- Look and hear— What's the problem? How did your child behave wrongly? Were you sure your child is wrong? Would you know? Is the behavior of your child normal for your child's age?
- Think— What are you trying to learn from your child? What can you do to assist your kid in self-management? What is your child's expectation?
- Act — considering the judgment.

Follow these steps to control anger;

- Count very gradually to ten. Think of the counting or something that makes you happy rather than the actions of your son.
- In your pants, place your hands. This will help you with intimidating your son or hurting him.
- Close your eyes. Take a reflective pause and gently let it go. Pretend that you release your body's steam.
- Get the situation away. Getaway. Take a walk in another house. Tell your partner, friend, or parent about your case. (Do this only if it is all right if your kid is alone or if there's someone to watch your child.)

TIMEOUT Rule

- "Time out" removes a child from a difficult or unpleasant situation to help relax the kid. Time out provides a chance to relax both kids and parents.
- Find a "time-out" location that is comfortable and secure. It should be away from other things and away from the misbehavior of your son.
- If your child tries to leave "time out" until he calms down, he returns the child softly and suggests, "When you are calm and ready to do something, you will return to play.
- Chat about why the "time out" is appropriate and what you foresee in the future when your child is happy. Say how the other child feels when your child harms another kid. Give your child a chance to console and apologize to the other person. Prepare how the kid should be in control in the future. Have the child take it up if something was knocked over. It helps the kid to change his or her behavior.
- Feel your child's affection when your attitude is relaxed, and your child returns to work quickly.
- Other parents decide to use a clock. Grant every year of your child's age one minute of "time out." The "time off," for instance, is 4 minutes if your kid is four years old.

- When kids grow older, they threaten to quit "time out" when able to do so. It makes a kid recognize when it's happy.
- It's all right to let you let your kid read a book or focus on a puzzle in the' time out' period.
- Encourage kids to invest their own time as they like. They will rest or split.
- "Time out" is often used for misbehavior by the child. "Time out" works for both parents and kids, as it calms both.
- Do not spend too much time away.
- Never use "time out" for children under three years of age.
- When a child is "time out," the parents must be quiet but firm.

"Time out" can be used for the avoidance of misconduct. Please ask your child to calm before a scenario gets out of control. Time out can also be used for the wrong behavior of an infant. This offers everyone a chance to renew themselves. You can discuss your problem with your child after "time off" is over.

CHAPTER 3: METHODS AND TECHNIQUES TO BUILD POSITIVE DISCIPLINE

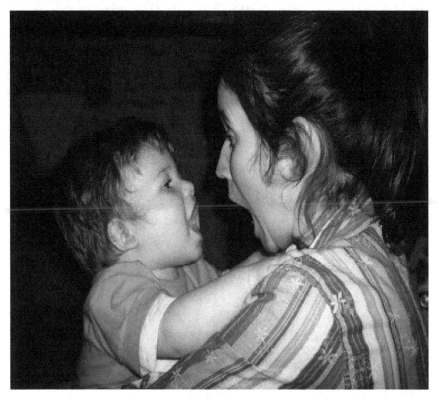

Persuasion Techniques The key to successful training is vocabulary and interaction. When disciplining children, a parent or teacher uses language patterns. We control the way children feel and think of our messages by influencing our comments to kids; by regulating how children feel and think about our news, we regulate their actions. Words and crafted letters carefully selected can actively create the mental images and mood necessary for kids to remove and comply more closely with noncompliance and oppositional behavior. If we convince children to behave, we regulate their actions employing words, use energy, not force. Sound reasoning training ensures that we can talk with the correct words to produce the desired results. Persuasive training includes clear language strategies and approaches to talk to kids about improving their emotional condition to facilitate behavioral change.

Persuasion Strategy: Take what You Want for Real

The kid may trust you if you speak and behave as though what you want. For starters, we send a message to the child as we believe something that he or she already needs to do what we inquire, stating, "Would your carrots or celery?" Assumes that one of these two vegetables the child wants and will consume.

Persuasion Strategy 1: Give Constructive directions

When we use constructive instructions, we follow more than when we use derogatory orders. Give Constructive directions. "Noise" or "Don't harm your younger brother" is degrading forms of guidance. Derogatory instructions tell kids what not to do. Positive directives, on the other side, tell children what to do to confirm. Work to change the negative directions to the favorable laws of your children. Shapiro (1994) advises that the derogatory instructions, which we generally suggest in one column, will be written down, and instead then the second column translates such words in a very different way and asks the kid what he will do. Also, give a positive explanation of what you want; for example, "Speak softly" instead of "Stop shouting."

Persuasion Strategy 3: pointing out an acceptable alternative

The child is directed by constructive guidance to more appropriate or similar actions. "To make noises at the table, bother people at diner, Shapiro gives the following details. You should take reason from the bed, and go for five minutes when you make noises, and then you have to go for a period because you reach your little friend. Use this pillow when you are upset, "Schaefer suggests (1994) that the child is more likely to modify the inappropriate behavior if we offer an acceptable alternative since he understands what he should do apart from what he should not.

Persuasion Strategy 4: Use More "Start" Messages and Fewer "Stop" Messages

It is easier to start than to stop. Use this principle when disciplining children; tell the children what to stop doing instead of telling them what to do. A teaching individual or a parent who understands how to behave in a constructive discipline may, for example, transform a statement, "Stop playing with that game" into "Please give me the toy." rather than always saying, "No" or "Stop it."

Persuasion Strategy 5: The term "start" can be substituted by "continue."

It is much easier to continue with an operation in motion than to begin anything new. The term "start" can be substituted by "continue" When you replace the word "begin" for that phrase, you will encounter fewer opposition to your application or order. Instead of suggesting, for instance, "Justin, start your homework" or "Justin, start reading your homework."

Persuasion Strategy 6: State Rules Impersonally

For example: "The policy in this school is not to wear a cap in a classroom" or "The rule here is not to move your mother" rather than "I like..." or "I hope to see..." When we use impersonal language, we are battling between the child and an impersonal law, not between the child and the parent or between two kids or children.

Persuasion Strategy 7: Give Alpha Commands

An order is a brief, authoritative assertion requiring immediate obedience. Two forms of instructions were described by Walker and Walker (1991).

- Beta commands involve vague and multiple directives, given simultaneously, and do not provide a clear compliance criterion. We do not share your child ample time and opportunity to meet with a beta order. In other terms, we do not advise the child precisely what to do to satisfy because we offer a beta command. Excessive verbalizations usually accompany beta instructions. A beta example is provided by Walker and Walker, "Jimmy, your room is always a mess! Why don't you purify it rather than wait for me?

- Alpha commands include a simple, explicit, and precise declaration without further verbalization and allow the child to reply within a reasonable period of five to 15 seconds. You instruct the kid precisely what to do; for instance: "Retrieve all items from the floor and put them on the shelf." Beta commands decrease adherence; alpha commands enhance compliance. Nonetheless, all forms of controls may be applied to a query, and we should thus use powers cautiously and only if appropriate. To send alpha commands, the authors recommend:

- Fair usage, concise terms, and conditions.

- Just give one command at a time, followed by a compliance period.

- Do not disagree with the child or give the child any order or control.

- Continue, starting with, "You must..." then saying a favorable outcome when the kid does not accomplish the same guidance.

- Once your child is in line with these values, show them positive attention and explanation of rewards, for instance, "Excellent, you replied promptly to what I told you to do."

Persuasion Strategy 7: More Requests and Fewer Commands

If a request does that, don't give a command. Always use more queries and proposals than direct orders or commands. By comparison to order, a question does not put pressure on it to comply; in other words, it gives the child the ability to decline. They ask questions in the form of social gatherings, such as' Can you please...?'" or' I like you...' (Walker and Walker, 1991). An application is requested; an order says. Unlike instructions, if you (Schaefer, 1994), you will have better results:

- Other than to inquire from a distance to stay close to the kid.
- Contact your eye.
- Limits yourself to two demands, never occasionally make the same request, and stop concurrently submitting multiple requests.
- Use a gentle yet firm voice to access the speech level.
- Instead of "stop" applications, using "run."
- Give the child a reasonable time (five to fifteen seconds) to satisfy your request.
- Make a clear, succinct query and optimistic wording; e.g., "Please turn off your lights,"
- A smile and "Thank You" align with the bonus.

Persuasion Strategy 9: Give Choices to the Child

It is essential to provide opportunities to improve positive behavior and children's adherence. Try to give the kid flexibility to choose, for instance, "Either play quietly or go upstairs to bed." Schaefer (1994) suggests that making choices is a means for kids to become more self-sufficient and make more decisions.

Persuasion Strategy 10: Use Forced Choices

We restrict our children's choices to only two to ensure the behavior we want. They term this strategy a "made selection" or "double obedience" because it still promotes the action they want, no matter what the kid wants to do. An example of a coerced choice is, "You have two options; either you go to bed now to have a story read to you, or after the TV show you go to bed." You will make the child easily choose the way that he desires and more challenging to select the less appealing alternative. You can also decide that the child wants more attractive and desirable. In our case, the parent increased the desirability of "right now" going to bed by including a child's special event in this choice; to read a story from her. If more than two options are available, have the first or last alternative for the kid. Forced decisions are other examples:

- Choices show, for instance, "Would you like your lunch for milk or orange juice... and lettuce... just or green peas...?" What fruit are you hunting for, pear or apple?"
- On Hierarchy, for instance,' Want to have a bigger or smaller ball?" What is the number of pages you'll read before the break?
- The option of comparison. You first propose something which the kid has very little hope of deciding, which makes it look probable. You follow the real solution, such as: "Right now, you can go to bed or get your things."

By making the child feel as though she is considering so, we will improve conformity with the decisions that have been made; one might say, "What do you do, wash the dishes or let the waste go??

Persuasion Strategy 11: Ask Leading Questions

It is imperative to address our main point in the form of a question, not a declaration. If we apply the leading information in the form of a request, we deter the child from being confused and coerced, and we send a message to the child. Furthermore, by answering deliberately designed questions that make the child trust in a particular way, we will improve the persuasive power of questions. Leading items include the response or point to which we seek to reply and push the child in the path we want. We delete any unnecessary alternatives when answering leading questions and take the child to the correct choice. Example are;

- Questions that create a hypothesis: for example, "how much will this year go up to your reading?" This means that this year's learning level increases. You pressure the kid to find the reading level first and only.

- Questions that relate everything you said earlier to what you have been saying are still in the kid's mind. "I felt honestly misled as we screamed, for starters. How are you doing softly speaking?

- Questions offering two options to make one choice more desirable, e.g., "Would you prefer to read here your book or in the quieter listening center?"–

- Questions are connecting the past to the future (cause and effect), for instance." If you go to bed late, what will happen in your math test tomorrow?"

- Questions that make the childcare of implications or repercussions, e.g., "If you hang out and Eric any time you get into trouble, what are you doing the next time you hang out the two of you? Last time, what happened?"

- Questions to which the kid responds." For instance, "Do you accept that we must discuss this matter? You can do this by saying what you want the child to consider and avoid saying something you want the child not to think about, such as "At this time we spoke, is it true that you feel calmer?

- Questions that have a positive effect on the child. Next, call the operation and then put the item in a manner which leads to child compliance, such as "Will you wash the dishes?" or "Can you help me move these boxes to the garage?"

Persuasion Strategy 12: Manipulate the Size of the Request to Make it Look Smaller or Bigger

You can do this in two ways:

- **Take the argument down (from smaller to larger).** Smaller systems are simpler to work with and recognize. With this technique, we are moving the child to make a more significant commitment by first asking for a smaller responsibility, i.e., to ask the child only to read five pages of the book and then to ask him to read the book. A change in this technique requires something small first, and when the child meets, we request something bigger and finally something larger; for instance, we are reading five pages and then the next ten pages, finished reading the book.

- **Consider the more significant (from larger to smaller) query first**. The purpose of breaking down our trust is this strategy. There, then, we request for something unreasonable and probably refuse, and if that child rejects, then we ask for something less challenging and more rational for the infant; in other terms, the first "no" is to be received, so that we can get a "yes" instead. For example, you ask the child to read the entire text and then through the query to just ten pages. By comparison, the second query tends to be less much quicker to respond to than the original request. Its technology uses the comparing concept.

Persuasion Technique 13: Buttering Up

Take into account the broader (larger or smaller) question. This technique is intended to break down our trust. We request something unfair there and probably refuse, so we ask for something less daunting for the baby if it is rejected and more rational; in other terms, we get the first' no' to get an a' yes' instead. For example, you ask the child to read the whole text first and then just ten pages through the question. Compared to the original question, the second query appears to be less straightforward. This utilizes the principle of contrast.

Persuasion Technique 14: Use Pauses

We may insert a break in a sentence or section to increase the argument's persuasive power in front of or after the critical message, recommendation, or order. A delay previous to the crucial point increases pressure (e.g., "Please... sit down") and reinforces this. Pause after the critical point (e.g.,' Please bring the game... before you lining up') helps the essential point sink down. Pause after offering an idea or order to the child will make the recommendation or instruction settle into the infant's head.

Persuasion Technique 15: Visualizing

If you want the child to feel a particular emotion, get it to remember when the feeling was experienced. For example, if you try to make a sad child happier or a frustrated child comfortable, make the child feel happy (or relieved), and then the new feeling removes the old surface. Dreaming or dreaming of a new, more positive sense allows the infant to step into your emotional state. Tell the child to remember a time when she knew harmony or joy, for instance, during the novel or a trip to the park, so that they can progress towards this happy or pleasant environment. You can suggest a moment and start describing the experience if the child has difficulty remembering. Ask the kid to ask who she does and what comes next in her head. To make the simulation more accurate, keep expanding the definition of the infant. The sensation associated with the memory is like suggestions that move the child into a new state when they recall the happy or calm memory. The memory recalls the pictures, and the images evoke a new feeling, i.e., imagine how happy or peaceful she was at that time makes her feel now delighted or calm. Pause between prints to give the child the time to watch the film in its mind to increase the visualization.

Persuasion Technique 16: Wondering

Wonder aloud about things that the child wants to do, believe, or accomplish. Check whether the kid will. Think about what may or may not have happened. Wonder what the benefits are. Wonder whether the kid knows still (e.g., quiet and relaxed). "When you unleash (e.g., feeling of rage or self-defeating) I say things like, 'I wonder what would happen.'"

Persuasion Technique 17: Use Odd Numbers

The pique strategy is also established. If we include an unusual number as part of the application, this leads to confusion and even question why we are applying so peculiarly. The second added mystery and curiosity brings compelling energy to the petition. "You can spare 19 dollars, for instance? "It's a quarter instead of telling. For children, claim, for example, that you want to get lights off and a child in bed at 9:23, or want the toys to be precisely 13 minutes after 2:00 on the stools. The child turns its focus to the strange time, which distracts it from declining.

Persuasion Technique 18: Linking

Link what the child needs do to something, such as "When you're (what you want) so you're going to get (or what a child wants)" Compare the action to something the child doesn't want; e.g., "When two of you start talking, you're going to have fewer screen time." The convincing link tells the kid the path back and the way to avoid what he needs.

Persuasion Technique 19: Use Repetition

Repetition is best employed and has an excellent supporting effect. Within our email, we will repeat the main words or phrases. The same words or phrases can be used during the massage; the keywords or phrases are the same, and the message is moving the child gradually into the directions we want. The key is the fact that the news is the same. Three basic repeating techniques are available; the third, the hammer, requires more language sophistication than the two first.

- **The three-fold method** helps us to emphasize the critical message. The triple can be three single words, three phrases, or three full sentences, but they must be three related items that match together to make a difference. The triple can be as easy as saying the same thing three times (e.g., "start" phrase or any other keyword repeated three times). In this example, each key message in the triple is also an overshadowed instance; you can say something like, "You are so cool, you seem willing to listen to my advice, talk about what happened, tell me which another choice you have had to solve this problem." Three elements in a series of three actions to achieve the objective can also be linked. We may alter our vocal tone (either up or down) to connect the triple more as we consider each essential item or move.
- **The jackhammer strategy** can be used to freeze and avoid dangerous behavior, especially during an emergency. We repeat three times and quickly with this process a single word or a short sentence. We are continually increasing our expression power, for instance, "no! No! No! NO! NO! Don't Hit Him! NO! NO! NO!! NO!!!"
- The hammer strategy tends to illustrate a specific subject in several sentences. In the following example, a teacher gives the class direction; he emphasizes the text, "You are learning." The first two chapters of the book will be read. You can read in 45 minutes, or you can read in one hour. You may ask your reader for help in finding a term that is difficult to pronounce, or if you want the definition of a new word, and I hope that we will be learning quicker than we anticipated. We have to read as quietly as we can to keep

other readers from interrupting and not to restart all chapters

Persuasion Technique 20: Use Power Sentences

They become more convincing when we use force expressions. At least one of the following elements is included in power phrases: ·

- Power phrases are quick to be hit. A paragraph or even a single sentence can be used in its entirety, e.g., "Begin now," or "Stile," and the infant takes the total sense of speech in a single step with a short sentence. A longer-term fuse with the background sound and the kid can skip the critical message. A simple word, easy to remember, three crucial elements of effective technique, is easy to understand.
- Power phrases use modal words, e.g., may, could, might, must, and will. We use modal verbs, depending on the text, to render it more or less significant. Power phrases utilizing feature verbs are bis. You should work alongside your learning buddy to find the meaning of the new vocabulary.
- Play Here; these sheets can be folded.
- You ought to support one another if you want to finish quicker.
- Ultimately, in one hour, you need to clean this place.
- Divide the power phrase into two sections to create interest, for example, "We will do... (speaking break) tomorrow... something very exciting! "The children receive a split sentence because they are interested in knowing how the sentence ends (Nitsche, 2006).
- Put the main effect at the end of a sentence (end impact) to optimize persuasive power, for example, "You can go to the math center now."

Persuasion Technique 21: Use Power Paragraphs

Most of all of the following items are included in a power section.

Few Sentences. Don't use too many phrases in a power paragraph; three or four names are appropriate.

Simple sentences. To explain and decide the text's conclusion, use the short phrase at the start of the section to grab the kids' attention and another short term at the end of the paragraph. Throughout comparison, after a long description or clarification, using short sentences to recap.

Pictorial explanations and tactile terminology. If we illustrate our expressions with images, sounds, and feelings, we instantly receive more attention and appreciation, strengthening our argument's persuasive strength. Instead of having the child understand the meaning (by analysis), tactile expression stimulates the brain's senses. Therefore, once a pictorial definition is used, we may create a solution with other objects, e.g., by a ladder, a brick wall (problem) (solution) can be scaled (Mahony, 2003). To order to help the infant use all three primary sensory modalities, a well-developed sensory message: (1) visual modality by scenario imaging; (2) hearing modalities

- Words of energy. Place one or two power terms in the email carefully for a more significant impact. Examples of power word are:
- Name or terms belonging to you, us, all, friends, team, us
- Terms stimulate excitement and motivate love, favorites, fascinating or interested; likes, sweeping or discovering, enjoying, fantastic, useful, profitable, challenge, major, wishes.
- Words that control behavior: convenient, quick, brief, or short
- Words that boost trust and confidence: right, good, assured, stable, sure, optimistic, trustworthy, solid
- Words of security: safe, safe, protected, protect, aid— final effect — now read, free, fast, precise, quick, short or short
- Words of trust encouraging. To optimize your article or message's compelling power, add a crucial point at the end: "For example, you need and to solve your word problems."

Persuasion Techni... 22: Use Hidden Commands

With this strategy, we cover the order from any control resistance; in other words, from the command resistance in the paragraph. Through modifying the sound of our voice, more precisely, we stress our secret order. We will adjust the sound of our voice because we signify the response we desire (verb). Secret order examples:

- **For example, I wonder Command** "I wonder if in 45 minutes you should arrange your closet?"
- **Doubt Command** We don't know if the child is in a position or willing to act with this command; for example, "can you reach this top shelf? Super! Super! Can you assist me in putting away these boxes?"
- **Assumption Command** There, we are behaving and speaking as though the child is obeying the order. We're acting here and talking as though the child would abide by the command. For example, "You want a glass of milk after you organize your closet?

Persuasion Technique 23: Use Proposals

Shaefer (1994) describes two main types of suggestions: – Indirect advice; for example, from what I understand, you believe it is better to let Cindy realize that she has to inquire before she takes the markers. A recommendation, for instance: You could want to talk about this or maybe you can do it in this way.

- **Implicit recommendations**; for example, 'You find the safest approach to fix it is to let Cindy realize she needs to remind you before she removes your markers.' A bit of implicit advice essentially confirms a notion that is already in the heads of a child.
- **Positive recommendations** are to give the child a positive quality even if the evidence that the child has the property or product is only nominal. We motivate the kid to act appropriately by implying how he works to some degree

already. Two examples: For yourself, you seem far more robust than ever, and I hope you will be courageous.

- You are best friends with Ricky, and I know you want him to resolve this matter.
- You're just a disciplined child at heart. You want your things to be easy, organized and identified.
- They, you don't give up, and you can seek to do your best.
- Positive interventions work best if the value of the infant we assign does not differ significantly from the character and capability of the child; in other terms, the kid will carry out the action or potential which we attribute to the child. The teacher uses constructive feedback to the tantric activities of a childcare professor in the following example:

Every day, you get stronger, wiser, and thoughtful. You're going to be so huge too early that the tanners are finished. Maybe next week, possibly by tomorrow you are so tall, or perhaps the next day, you can reassure yourself, "No, I won't get angry when you get another son. Tomorrow, "I'm not going to get a tantrum because I" am a great girl today. There're no big girls with tannins. That's what small children do. You say, "I'll be a big girl," and you stay away from trouble. Yes, honey, you're growing big and bright, and soon the tannins will disappear... the tannins are going to disappear... just go away.

Persuasion Technique 24: Establish Rapport

The more kids think you are friends, the more they'll like you and will hear what you've got to say. As an outsider, we have a limited influence, but as a trustworthy friend who knows what we can do. When the child trusts us and likes us, our conviction is far more manageable. The ability to generate reactions in the infant is to achieve and maintain connexions. Unlike dance partners, people mirror in partnership and fit in place and movement (the body's complimentary language). The best thing to do is make an overall mood and actions close to the spirit and behavior of the kid by deliberately imitating main habits and the like;

- Breathing ability to suit (rate or depth) to breathe harmony
- Mirroring motions, including actions of hands and feet
- Matching speech (blending and harmonizing), i.e., tempo, tone, or rhythm
- Representing a standard motion style; for example, how rapidly and how many movements of the hands and legs are open or locked (i.e., arms and legs are crossed)
- copying the head orientation
- Replicated pose of an infant, e.g., sitting, upright, or leaning back
- Lying on the same component (your right to the left of the child) to create the same balance and distribution of body weight
- Exchange suit; we use some part of the body to fit the tempo; for example, we are making a gesture like taping the hand to match the infant's breathing pattern. When raising a leg or hand up and down correctly, we will fit the child's breathing rhythm. We can also suit the gestures of our hands to hand motions and head motions with body motions

Persuasion Technique 25: Use Mirroring and Exchanged Matching

We create a relationship that is central to influencing and persuaded children by reflecting and exchanging matches. By subtly mirroring or modifying those immediate actions to convince the infant, we establish an emotional state close to the child's emotional state.

- The mirroring method replaces the child's body language and speech (speed, tone, volume, or rhythm) (facial expression, expressions, pacing, stance, or movement). We may conduct our reflections concurrently or slightly later, without the copying of the boy. That is why we advise that you only look at some critical steps and chosen times; if you cross your hands, for instance, you do the same thing; if you shorten, we shrink; if you talk fast, we talk fast. When you speak rapidly, we sputter.

- The substitute game is a mirroring process. We synchronize body language or speech with this neuro medical strategy, but without copying the infant explicitly. For, e.g., if the child is crossing his arms, we are crossing our beings; if the child scratches his face, we rub one arm; if the child coughs, we clear our throat. We can also use some parts of the body to match rhythms, for example, by shifting one leg according to a fast breathing pattern.

Persuasion Technique 26: Use a Matched Dictionary or Matched Language

According to Mahony (2003), when using the chosen representation method (visual, auditory, kinesthetic, or tactile) for children, our connexions and mutual understanding are enhanced. In simple words, we enhance interactions as we "speak the language of the infant." Predicates are sensory words and phrases, implying that predicates are messages that link directly to our senses, feelings and not with our brains (reasons and analyses). They often do not realize that our words and phrases are geared towards one particular auditory representative method and that by merely speaking with kids with their interests, not ours, they can communicate better to them.

A misguided speech illustration is:

Child: in my head, I can look into it. I realize that I will miss the spelling test.

Parent (kinesthetics predicate): Hold on a second. You have learned (kinesthetically) intensely and understand specific terms in writing.

— Definitions of the related language:

Child: I can't understand the things I have to do with this map.

Teacher: Oh, what do you think is the (kinetic) problem? Kid: I'm going to curse if I like it (kinetic prediction)!

Persuasive Technique 27: Pace and Lead

We get a rhythm and the leading strategy from neurolinguistic literature (Vaknin, 2008; Nitsche, 2006; O'Connor and Seymour, 2002). This method comprises four steps: the child's location is mirrored or balanced by movements, choice of words, speech, or respiration. The second step is to mimic the child to link. The third step is to move with the child for a time, and at the same speed before trying the fourth and final step, leading the child to the psychic and psychic status, we want to convince us and help us better receptively. Also, we link up with the infant and improve the interaction by mirroring in the pacing stage; in the first step, we adjust our physiology and attitude to change the child's physiology and philosophy. Leading is not sufficient without a well-established relationship, so before we try to lead the infant, we will take our time to link and communicate with the child in time.

They then look at the movements and the main actions chosen to suit how the child feels. Then we gradually turn the mirrored behavior into a positive and resourceful state, such as breathing speed and body language, which push your child into the new government. Three examples will be provided below to transform an unhappy and anxious infant, utilizing pacing and leading software, into an optimistic and calmer state.

- Synchronize the heart speed quicker, and increase it slowly so that the infant's movement is more massive and slower; relaxed physiology.
- Frown the baby, cross your arms, lean back, and hold your palms shut (closed body position). Lay your face off, unfold your arms, sit back, open your palms, and move closer to the child. Gradually, move towards an open and inviting posture.
- Do a game for the mood (Mahony 2003), which balances the child's strength with his rage. At the outset of this

process, the author recommends demonstrating your "energy level" as high as your child's energy level but not more excellent. Yet, you express your power as a positive emotion like desire or worry. Displaying a calmer tone of voice and showing fewer and quicker body movements, for instance, will slowly change the energy level downward.

Persuasion Technique 28: The Voice Regulation Method

We have the legislative speech strategy from Nitsche (2006). Teachers and parents often feel we need to talk more and more loudly to get kids to hear what we are talking about and get kids to do what we want them to do. Furthermore, by increasing our speech's strength, we can monitor (increase or lower) the level of children's voices. To stop a noisy, angry boy, for instance, take the following steps:

- Your words first have to be more apparent than the sounds of the boy. It produces an element of surprise, and the child becomes silent.
- Speak split. We'll teach the kid what we think of her by stopping and being quiet.
- 3. Continue to murmur. It makes the child more vigilant and more responsive.
- 4. Continue speaking and change the normal tone from whispering.

We use very few terms with this strategy to demonstrate to the infant the action we want from it (display; do not say the technique). In the following examples, the same voice control method was modified for use with a loud group by Nitsche (2006)

- Do not say a word if the class sees you as you enter the classroom. Freeze your attitude and get in contact with your brain. Hold this mentality and resist the temptation to talk. You encourage the group to remain silent by being silent. You have to use your speech or bright ring to get the class to see you if they don't hear you. Use the same solution in this scenario.

- Keep the body straight and stop. Keep your feet straight and turn to each other so that the weight is evenly balanced on both sides. Extend a hand to your side and keep it parallel to the floor; you also have a frozen eye. Tell,' GOOD MORNING LADIES' (voice clearer than the size of the class) and' Gentlemen' We're going to start now!"You always whisper this final sentence and then float to the average strength of your speech.

Persuasion Technique 29: Use Discipline Anchors

A signal is an object that always responds the same way. The answer can either be an intervention (can be seen) or a shift in a state of mind (attitude) or psychological (feeling). An anchor can be anything we want; a frozen posture, for example, holds one arm and says, "Stop!"To point at an ear to sign to a child to listen, count from five to one, place a green hat on, or tap into the plot. If the same Signal, Theory, or concept is provided frequently and consistently, the Signal and Event are related or attached. The anchor generates positive anticipation, leading to a change in inner state from restless to attentive by putting on a green hat. The "It's time to tell the story!" The more we use a sure anchor, the quicker the children reply to that anchor (Nitsche 2005, 2006). Anchors are reflexes, involuntary responses that we create without the word or with very few words. We realize that when we see children reacting to our desires without using the terms, we have built an important anchor.

Persuasion Technique 30: Use Space Anchors

An equally powerful strategy in school and at home is the placement of several anchors in different places. (Nitsche, 2006), or where the child is at home, in other rooms. Once we reach one of these spaces, kids know what is happening next without terms. Nitsche recommends the following space anchors for teachers (parents can adjust to their home using fewer anchors):

- **Admonishment spot**, freeze the stance, move to the scene, stand upright, and see the perpetrator without saying a word.
- **The Caution Anchor** is where the teacher is standing at the beginning of the lesson to get class attention. You have to use the second place of emphasis to focus during the course; for example, in front and middle of the classroom.
- **Learning spot**, the location where the teacher shares information. When you move towards this place, gradually and suddenly, children will see and be more conscious.
- **The spot of storytelling** put on a green hat or any other visual cue, and go there. Share your story or event once there.
- **The Quiet Spot** is the spot to mark total silence.
- **The Spot of Hot Tips**, make a large "X" on the board, facing the space with a masking tape. Explain with children what you intend to see every time you step in, how they take the hot tips, that is, lean forward and listen carefully with open eyes. You only share essential information at the hot tips spot. So soon as the kids are in hot tips, you say the hot end dramatically.
- **The Discipline Anchor,** the anchor, should be next to where you post the classroom rules. You can stand inside this place each time you discipline the class or a particular kid. Nitsche (2006) alerts us that we never stand on the discipline anchor during a different activity. Furthermore, everything related to education, such as books or crayons or any other action, must be put down during discipline. You also need to breathe calmly. Speak not more than one sentence or phrase within this anchor, for example, a simple command, like "You've got to," then leave the anchor discipline and continue to teach or interact with the child as if nothing happened.

Each "new" anchor from the other is significant. For example, we use the same spot to deliver homework if we have the homework anchor, and we don't use this spot for anything else. We can also corrupt an anchor if we give incongruous signals to kids, for example, when you are already in a quiet position, then keep talking, or gesturing the' low your tone' symbol (hand palm down and lowered by degrees) while increasing our volume and shouting. Instead, if you use a green hat to indicate storytime, you don't use the same cap as the signal,' go online. We are already standing in the silent place, so we continue speaking, or we point at a sign "Drop Your Voices." But we are raising our volume and yelling. When we properly use it, it can be a useful motivating tool consistently and "cleanly."

Persuasion Technique 31: Get a Pledge from the Child

Children are more likely to make changes in their actions when they talk and pledge to themselves, so after you always close your query by saying, "Will you do so?